Will's World

Through the Eyes of His Family and Friends

MARGERY MATHIS HENDERSON

Order this book online at www.trafford.com
or email orders@trafford.com

Most Trafford titles are also available at major online book retailers.

Printed in the United States of America.

ISBN: 978-1-4669-6209-5 (sc)
ISBN: 978-1-4669-6210-1 (hc)
ISBN: 978-1-4669-6211-8 (e)

Library of Congress Control Number: 2012918380

Trafford rev. 11/17/2012

 www.trafford.com

North America & international
toll-free: 1 888 232 4444 (USA & Canada)
phone: 250 383 6864 ♦ fax: 812 355 4082

DEDICATIONS

First I dedicate this book to Will, whose life is lived everyday for others. His faith, motivation and determination are my inspiration.

To my late husband, William Glenn Henderson, Will's "Aundie," who was determined that Will reach the heights for which God had created him.

To my Daughter, Cindy Henderson Hurt, who is the best person I know and my hero.

To all of you who have made a loving contribution to Will's life, I lovingly dedicate this book to each of you.

ACKNOWLEDGEMENTS

Without the contributions from those of you who have written, both lengthy and brief, tributes to Will, this book could not have been written. To each of you I want to express my heartfelt gratitude. Most of all I want to thank you for your part in making Will's life a "book" from which each of us can learn.

I especially wish to recognize Sue Stivers, Nancy Brewington, Connie Duvall, Judge John Alexander, Rebakah Burns, Alisa Baker, Pauline Roberts, Johnny Sells, and Patricia Thomas. Each of you has taken the time and effort to show Will of your love, patience and determination to see that his life is filled with meaning and purpose. His family joins me in thanking each of you.

I also wish to thank Jo Murley for writing both Foreword and Afterword. Both are beautiful and inspirational as only Jo could have written.

FOREWORD

Having known members of Will Hurt's family since my salad days and having known Will, himself, since his birth, I am both honored and humbled to pen the foreword to this beautiful book. Written by his maternal grandmother, Will's story comes alive in the hands of a woman who knows and loves him so well.

When Will comes to mind, I can't help but recall a quote by Lou Holtz which reads, "I don't believe that God put us on earth to be ordinary." In his extra-ordinariness, Will Hurt exemplifies anything but a light dimmed by atypical autism with which he was diagnosed during his teen-age years. His ambition and determination to be the best he can be, his drive to expand horizons and leap the limitations imposed by society and many professionals, culminate in Will's being a-typical in the very best of ways.

Jo Murley
Feature Columnist
Cumberland County News
Burkesville, Kentucky

CHAPTER 1

Will's Birth

Cindy's eyes were filled with fear as she walked from her obstetrician's office and with a trembling voice she quietly spoke to her mother, "The doctor says I must go directly to the hospital and be prepared for a cesarean section. He said I have developed toxemia, and he wants to take the baby right away." Cindy's mom had driven her to her appointment that morning, because it was to have been a very routine visit with no unforeseen complications. This was July, 1990, and with summer break, Cindy's other two children, Scott and Holly were with them and Cindy's mother was concerned that they not become fearful and upset.

Cindy was insistent that Steve be with her for the surgery. When called from his judicial duties he rushed to Cindy's side at the hospital in Glasgow, Kentucky. Cindy's father had also arrived to be with his family. The doctor restated his concern for both mother and child, Steve, along with her parents sat anguished as Cindy was wheeled into surgery. The doctor's frightening words, "toxic" and "life-threatening" hung over us like a veil of terror. By this time we knew that Cindy was suffering from toxemia and that her baby was breach. Would Cindy survive? Would this precious baby survive?

The interminable wait was broken by the great news: Miraculously mother and child both had survived and were in recovery. Steve rushed to be with his radiant wife and son. Her parents sighed with relief, tearfully hugged and gave thanks for their now three healthy grandchildren.

Scott and Holly were ecstatic in welcoming home their new baby brother. His parents named him William Glenn Hurt to honor both of his grandfathers, William Hildreth Hurt and William Glenn Henderson. He soon became "Will" which today ironically fits with his optimistic personality and strong determination.

Although Will was frail, he was a beautiful baby in every way. Cindy soon became concerned that he seemed to sleep far than his brother and sister had. Often she had to wake him to be fed. She was troubled by the notion that Will's development was not proceeding normally.

Will continued to make progress and turned over in his crib at about six months of age. With support at his back he could sit up at nine months of age. We celebrated when he walked independently as he was nearing his second birthday. With a very limited vocabulary he began to talk between two and three years of age.

Our precious Will was very lethargic with low muscle tone. As stated earlier in his infancy he would often sleep for twelve to fifteen hours without waking and often would need to be roused in order to give him his bottle. Always there was a solemn look or expression on Will's face with few "normal" facial expressions. He was non responsive to stimuli.

Will was fed by bottle for quite a long time because of a gagging reflex when introduced to new foods with different textures.

When Will was 22 months old and still was unable to walk totally independently, his pediatrician referred us to the Child Evaluation Center (now known as the Weisskopf Child Evaluation Center) in Louisville, KY. This was because of her concerns of Macrocephaly and delayed motor development.

On June 21, 1991 he was seen by Dr. Hersh of the Child Development Center as a referral for Macrocephaly and developmental delays. A diagnosis from that visit found hypotonia with more left sided involvement. When the doctor did activities with Will such as swinging him through the air, Will would draw up his left side which indicated low muscle tone on his left side, which goes hand in hand with low stamina. Some of the additional diagnostic "impressions" from that visit were as follow:

➤ Developmental delay with greatest deficits in gross motor skills and less significant language and fine motor skills
➤ Relative macrocephaly

➤ Oral motor hypersensitivity
➤ Heart murmur—probably innocent
➤ R/O Sotos syndrome, fragile X syndrome (later proved negative)

On July 16, 1991 we received test results for Fragile X syndrome which involves a chromosome study. Will did not have any evidence of the syndrome.

Will was seen again by Dr. Hersh in June of 1992. The hypotonia was thought to be improved. Preschool and speech/language were encouraged.

His progress at age 23 months was as follows:

• Developmental delays with greatest deficits in gross motor abilities
• Using a few single words, and understanding simple commands
• Able to identify a few body parts and indicating his needs through gestures
• Began walking independently at this time
• Able to stack blocks, ride a push toy, and climb up and down stairs
• Using a fork and spoon, and using a straw
• Expressive language deficits

Will was evaluated by a number of institutions and specialists in Child Development, including Children's Hospital in Louisville, Kentucky and Vanderbilt Children's Hospital in Nashville, Tennessee. His final and perhaps most accurate diagnosis was Atypical Autism.

In Will's early years he avoided eye contact. He had and still has a keen sense of hearing. He would become very uncomfortable when exposed to loud noises such as fireworks, lawn equipment, loud voices and did not enjoy birthday parties with his friends. Will preferred to play alone, and was most comfortable with an adult family member. His choices of activities were always routine, repeating the same phrases time after time. In his grandparent's house was a low round table and, since Will preferred to play the same games over and over, he and his grandmother spent hours "driving" a tiny blue toy car round and round the table never varying the routine. On that same round table they spent hours playing the TV game show WHEEL OF FORTUNE.

When his grandmother would come to his home to pick him up to go to her house there was a pasture of horses along the way. He knew cows which were on his parent's farm but was unfamiliar with other animals. He was then about two years of age. Each time his grandmother would ask him to tell her what those animals were and he would say, "Cow". She would say, "That is a horse." He would then repeat, "Cow". As time went on NaNa, as Will called her, would repeat the same question as they passed that pasture. He would say, "Cow horse".

When he was just past two he had learned to slowly descend his grandparent's basement steps where his grandfather kept his home office. His grandfather, whom he was named for, kept a computer on his desk. "Aundie", as Will called him, taught him to access his e-mail and explained to Will how the message came from another place to his computer. Will was "hooked" on computers. Each time he came into his grandparent's house he would head to the basement, repeating these words, "I am going to check Aundie's mail from the sky." This was in 1992-93. His grandmother did not know how to access "mail from the sky" but Will did and his knowledge and love for computers has only grown through the years. Will had found his passion which now includes cell phones. He is everyone's in-house tech and is free to everyone who needs his advice. His first business cards read, "No Bill Will".

At about four years of age, Will told NaNa that we needed to tell someone the directions to a popular lake resort near us. NaNa suggested that the two of them draw a map for them. He became intrigued with maps and every time the two of them were just going from his house to his grandparent's, they followed the map they had drawn. When anyone casually mentioned that they were going to make a trip he would say, "We can make a map".

When Will was just over one year old, his parents asked NaNa if she would keep Will while they took his older brother and sister to the Louisville zoo for the day. She gladly obliged. Not wanting Will to totally miss a trip to the zoo, NaNa devised a plan. In his grandparents' house there were carved deer which they had brought from Switzerland, carved elephants from having lived in Africa, bears brought from Alaska, and other carvings and pictures of animals from around the world. When NaNa asked him if he wanted to go to the zoo, he smiled. He and his grandmother got crackers from the kitchen to feed the animals and they were off to their private zoo. They stopped to talk and feed all of the animals in his grandparents' twelve room house, including the second floor. When they became tired and needed to go "home" and rest, Will took a long nap as NaNa planned the remainder of their trip. When Will awoke we wrote a story of "Will's first trip to the zoo". He helped NaNa remember the names of the animals they had seen and the ones they had fed and the story remains in "Will's Book".

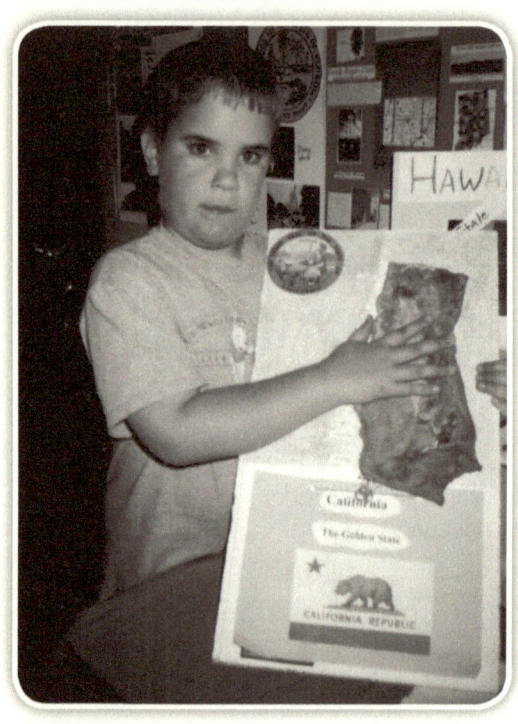

When Will was in the lower elementary grades his grandmother asked the Special Education Director, after her evaluation of him, what we might expect of his progress. Her reply was this, "If Will's academic abilities takes him to a fourth grade level I will be very surprised".

Will's grandparents had taken his older brother and sister too many countries and events outside of the US. They were planning to leave for the United Kingdom where they would reside for two years. Being sad that they had never been able to take Will on these trips, they planned his first flight to Disney World in Florida.

Sensing that this was a special event for both grandparents and grandson, the Captain of the Plane invited Will into the cockpit even placing his hat on Will's head. During that momentous trip, his grandfather taught Will to swim, "play tennis" and several other first time activities. Later on Will, along with his parents, brother and sister visited his grandparents in England where the fun and learning continued. When he became too tired to walk he found the shoulders of his father or grandfather. Once when his parents looked from their London hotel window they spied both grandfather and grandson at the top of a very tall trapezoid.

We began to notice that from everyone Will seemed to bring out their kindness and gentle spirit. He would be frightened of the sound of a storm and always there was a classmate or teacher who would make their way to sit beside him until the storm passed. Once when Will was in the barber's chair receiving a haircut and his grandmother was sitting along the wall waiting, a popular politician came into the shop. This politician was not known for kindness or gentleness. He stepped hurriedly past the grandmother with barely a nod. When he was in front of Will he stopped, smiled, called him by name and chatted as it Will were the person he had come to see. To herself the grandmother remarked, "Anyone who can bring this kind and gentle spirit from this politician has to have very special gifts".

Will's father, Steve Hurt, is a KY Senior Judge so Will has become very special in Kentucky Judicial circles. He attends all conferences with his father whether his father is teaching, leading or just attending these conferences. His popularity was made very evident about three years ago. Steve was to lead a Judicial College at Lake Barkley Lodge, some four hours from his home. Will remained with his mom, Cindy, and they were shopping in Bowling Green, KY. When Steve walked into the conference center from the judges assembled there came a chorus, "Where is Will"? Steve drew a deep breath and answered, "He didn't come". The judges replied, "Then you go and get him. We cannot start without Will". Steve called Cindy and told her that he must come for Will and asked her if she could meet him at a halfway point. Will was so excited and found it hard to keep his hands calm as he said, "They need me. I can't believe it. They really need me". Now there is no question Will attends every judicial conference even attending many where his father is not required to attend. He has done an internship at the Administrative Office of the Courts in Frankfort, KY, the State Capitol.

After high school he was accepted at a local college where he completed a technology class which has better equipped him to assist people with their computers and cell phones.

The longtime UCLA basketball coach, John Wooden, once said, "Never let what you can't do interfere with what you can do". Will lives that every day. He lives to volunteer. His two main concerns in life are, "What am I going to do on the days that I have no place to volunteer" and the other, "What will I do when I must retire". We tell him that he doesn't need to have either of these worries.

In October, 2006 a psychological report was completed on Will during his 10th grade year in high school. At that time, his full scale IQ was determined to be a 52.

For those of you who may have a special child in your family this book is written to encourage you that with early intervention, family, friends, school and plenty of motivation there is no limit to the contribution this child can make to our world. Every day Will touches more lives in a personal positive way than anyone can imagine. He touches lives face to face, on his cell phone, I Pad, and computer. He is often referred to as their "tech genius".

Many of Will's family members, friends, and teachers asked if they might write something to be included in WILL'S

WORLD. Following are those comments along with their names and how they have been, and continue to be, a part of his life. Some are e-mail messages which he has sent and received.

Will is very creative and loves rewarding others. This is an e-mail exchange with his friend, Sue Stivers. "Hi Sue. I think you and I need to write a little book about Phyllis Smith and tell all she did for Burkesville, KY". Phyllis was recently deceased and was a good friend of both Sue and Will. Sue's reply, "Will, that is a great idea! We need to start writing down all of the things we know that she did. Also we could ask some other people who knew her longer than we did. Let's make this our project! Thanks for the idea . . . it's a really great one! Sue had just "made his day" as she does very often. Sue is Executive Director of Columbia-Adair County Chamber of Commerce in KY and one day each week Will proudly volunteers as her office helper.

Very quickly Will asked his grandmother, NaNa, to be involved in this book project and this is NaNa's e-mail to Will, "Will, I think it is great that you want to write a book about Phyllis. She was a great friend to you and to so many other people. I am sure Sue feels the same way about Phyllis. They were great friends. Maybe it is a little too soon to write a book since Sue is so busy and you are going to begin golf lessons. You also are helping to plan your family reunion and planning for the big Fred Capps Memorial Golf Tournament. Have Mom or Scott help you write a letter to Lombeh and I will put your letter in the book I am writing about Lombeh. Your letter could be in the book as Mom's and Sue's will be. Do you think that is a good idea?" Signed, "I love you", NaNa

Sue shared Will's request and excitement with Will's grandmother, NaNa. Following is her reply to Sue concerning this desire of Will. "Sue, as much as I am with Will, he has never voiced any of this to me. I had no idea that these thoughts were inside him Will expresses in writing what he is unable to express in person to person. That is often a trait of autism. A few years ago I was at Notre Dame University to hear a well-known speaker, Temple Grandin. She one of the best known professional autistic persons in the country. She, at that time, was teaching at Colorado State University and has become a specialist in understanding and dealing with animals.

She has a PHD and has written a number of books relating to autism. In her lecture she told of how she had no idea how to interact socially. She told us that she could not feel human emotions herself but would sometimes react to someone else's emotions. I remember a few years ago when our family was attending an uncle's funeral service. Will was sitting between his mother and me. He had sat there without any sign of emotion until he looked up and saw tears coming from his mother's eyes. Tears then started rolling down his cheeks but it was if he did not know what to do with them.

I think Will has a book inside of him that only he can write and someday he and I shall do that".

Will often volunteers in various state and local offices. One of his favorite places is in Nancy Brewington's office who is Cumberland County Circuit Court Clerk. Nancy thrills him with the poems she writes about him.

Nancy writes, "Will this is just because I am thinking of you poem

In 1990, on Thursday, July 19.

Little Will came on the scene.

A little brother for Holly and Scott,

Just one look and they loved him non-stop.

He may have been little but he was loud,

And Mom and Dad were, Oh, so proud!

He grew and became a wiz with computers and phones,

And if you need any help, he's one you can rely on.

I value him as a friend and nothing to him I'd begrudge,

And he'll always be considered my 'Little Judge'."

Several years later Nancy writes another poem for Will.

"I'm sitting here a-doodling, cause this p.m. court is a bore;

So while I am thinking about you, I'm writing you a poem once more.

Christmas has come and gone, Will, my dear;

And now we look forward to a brand new year.

A new computer and new cell phone;

So that we can either call or e-mail home.

We program them in the morning and all day through;

To keep in touch with all, me and you.

We put numbers in and take addresses out;

That's what computers and cell phones are all about.

I know for a fact, Will, that with both of the above you're a pro;

And I can always ask you if there's something I need to know.

I really need a new phone, so on you I'll probably call;

Cause about these new fangled phones I know nothing at all.

They take pictures and talk and with all those buttons to use;

Mostly they just keep me totally confused!

I'll probably push the wrong button and end up on Neptune;

I'll need to call you, Will, to bring me back at least to the moon.

Then bring me on down, down, down with all of your worth;

So I'll finally end up back here on earth.

Thank you, Will, for being my friend;

One that I know, on whom I can always depend.

Several of Will's former elementary, middle and high school teachers, friends and extended family were invited to share their insight concerning Will's development. Some of those will be shared here.

"Will is a super special young man who has blessed my life since he was my student in 2ⁿᵈ grade

He has the determination to succeed from whom we all can and should learn". Paulette Andrews, Cumberland County Schools

"William Glenn Hurt has touched my life in many, many positive ways but one memory in particular stands above the rest. As a nine or ten year old fifth grader, Will knew so much more about my cell phone than I could ever hope to know! He was able to teach me many things about my cell phone. I use that knowledge even today . . . ten years later. Thanks, Will. You are my personal technological genius!"

Emily Allen, Cumberland County Elementary Faculty Member

"Will has always been a joy to be around. He always makes me smile and is always a willing volunteer. During the years that I was Cumberland County Elementary School Principal, he would occasionally come after he was finished at the high school and answer the phone for us. He enjoyed every minute of this volunteer task. Will is exciting to be around at the Fred Capps Memorial Golf Tournament each fall, patrolling in his special golf cart and keeping us under control. He loves being a member of the Planning Committee." Rodney Schwartz, DPP/Intervention Specialist Cumberland County Schools

"Don't let what you cannot do interfere with what you can do." John Wooden

On December 6, 2011 Will received this letter.

Will Hurt, Department of Court Services Intern

Frankfort, Kentucky

"Will, I would like to take this opportunity to extend an official welcome to you as the newest Department of Court Service intern. With approval from the Director's Office being granted for your intern position yesterday, Ms. Roberts and I will be talking about the tasks that you will work on for Education and possibly other divisions within the Department of Court Services.

We are excited to have you on board and will contact you next week with a list of duties.

Thank you for your willingness to volunteer your time with us.

Sincerely,

Deborah Williamson, AOC

Below is another tribute to Will from Nancy Brewington, Circuit Court Clerk, Cumberland County, KY

"Will, you have touched my life in so many ways. You kindness and willingness to help in any situation is beyond compare. You were so very helpful to me when you volunteered to work in my office and helped each of us with applications for drivers' license, filing citations and running errands always with a smile on your face.

When I needed to go to Frankfort, our State Capitol, for orientation and there was snow you became concerned for my safety. You suggested to your father that the two of you take me there in his truck.

You are always thinking of other people which tells all of us that you are a remarkable young man with a bright future."

In June, 2007, after taking Driver Education classes in high school Will was ready to apply for his driver's license. He was seventeen years of age and had practiced for many years, first with the family golf cart, then a four wheel farm vehicle and then farm equipment. To celebrate this milestone another poem from his friend, Nancy.

"He got his driving permit, did William Glenn,

And I am so very proud of him.

Now take care of it and drive real good;

Wear your seatbelt; don't speed, like a safe driver should.

Look left and right everyday,

Make sure it is clear from either way.

Don't hit the gas and spin around,

If you're driving in our little town

The Law will catch you; the time will be short,

Then you will end up in your Daddy's court.

The speech he will give you will last a long time,

And you will still end up paying a big, fat fine.

Your insurance will go up and your confidence will go down,

You'll see the Law everywhere in this town.

They are here, they are there, and they are everywhere,

They are even in your rear view mirror.

All kidding aside, I know you'll drive quite swell,

And give credit where due, 'Mother taught me real well'

So congratulations, I know you'll drive safe and meek,

And always watch out for other drivers on Allen's Creek."

Recently Will was asked by Patricia Thomas who is a local attorney to do research for a legal opinion she is working to complete. Will was thrilled that she trusted him to do this and following are her comments concerning her association with Will.

"The first time I noticed Will was at one of our local restaurants. He was with his grandmother and they were sitting across the restaurant from me waiting for their lunch to be served. His grandmother was working, ever so patiently with Will, encouraging him as he read a book. The patience which his grandmother demonstrated was amazing. What was even more amazing was the fact that Will was trying just as hard to read and together they were succeeding.

The next biggest hurdle crossed that I was aware of was when Will obtained his driver's license. Knowing that his Grandfather Hurt had arranged for him to drive his golf cart through the fields from his home to the grandparents' was also amazing. Then I learned that Will (and I am sure with a great deal of help from his family) not only was able to pass the written part of the driver's test, but successfully completed the road test. As I understand it, when Will came in with his REAL DRIVER'S LICENSE IN HIS HAN, PICTURE AND ALL, it not only made both parents very happy, but the wealth of pride in his accomplishment was beyond words.

As time has passed, I have been tracking Will's endeavors throughout the years. Nancy Brewington as Cumberland Circuit Clerk has praised his work and effort at the Cumberland Circuit Clerk's Office. I have also been impressed by reading about his volunteer work at Barren County Circuit Clerk's Office in Glasgow, Kentucky and Administrative Office of the Courts in Frankfort, Kentucky.

Knowing that I needed someone that (1) I could trust and understood that those matters related to law had to be kept in strictest confidence, and (2) someone who would be able to accomplish the task independent of my direction after I explained what I needed, and (3) could work at his own pace without needing my constant supervision, I approached Will with the task which needed to be done.

At our initial meeting I explained what need to be done. We went on line, opened one of the folders, or group sets, of WC Opinions and Awards, clicked onto one of the individual Opinions and Awards that needed to be reviewed in research and the current standard of the Worker's Compensation Law, and printed out that document. With first project successfully completed, we returned to the Group Set home page.

Knowing that it was a period of over seven months that needed to be tackled, with multiple opinions (if not weekly, then bi-weekly) from the Worker's Compensation Board and the Court of Appeals, and in order to keep it streamlined, Will and I together worked out a system. I would e-mail to Will directly those items which need to be downloaded. Will then created a time sheet/spread sheet to keep track of his hours and so the project began.

Will works at his own pace as he has many volunteer commitments to continue. He does meticulous work, which is so tedious and more often than not very boring. He is ever mindful to let me know when copy paper or printer ink is running low. Not many people would have either the time, patience or desire to tackle each opinion. Then there is the task at keeping them straight as to date of official publication and in order of date/time publication. Will then separates each opinion, grouping sets with colored pages. He then moves on to the next group set of opinions to be addressed. One must also be aware that, in the beginning, Will had to work backwards in tackling each group set of opinions.

I realize that I am the winner in this working relationship. I have someone that I can trust to keep the work assignments confidential, produce a quality product, which has been efficiently completed, without my having to hover and take time from my other practice. Will has become acutely aware from working in the Circuit Clerk's offices, working with his father, Senior Judge Steve Hurt, and working at AOC Offices that confidentiality and discretion are foremost in working with anything remotely related to the law.

This is one of the most reassuring aspects of working with Will. In the past when I had employees working there were two, and only two rules that were never to be broken. One, whatever you hear, see, type, copy or print concerning any clients or matters of law stays in this office. Two, never lie to me or steal from me, or do anything or do anything outside the office that would reflect negatively on this practice. With Will both concepts are already instilled in him and did not need to be addressed. With Will both concepts are a given. His handshake is the binding contract between him and me. He is amazing in his approach to each assigned task and living proof that a person does not have limitations that is respected for their proven abilities.

Yes, one can say that downloading published opinions from Worker's Compensation Board and Court of Appeals hardly merits confidentially. The confidentiality and discretion come from undertaking the task for the Law Firm in the beginning. I do not ever need to have any concern about Will's work product, his work ethic, his temperament in dealing with 'the stressed out lawyer' or wonder when or if he will complete a task or project. When he calls and tells me that the next 'set' of opinions is finished, upon presenting the finished pages, his smile completely melts all of the stress I have built during the busy day. His pride, upon presenting the finished product to me, definitely proves and renews my faith that I made the right choice in having Will undertake the project. As I said, I am the fortunate one"

"Will is living proof of the hope that today is a blessing and tomorrow an adventure."

The author of this book recently received this e-mail from Will which reads, "I am sending something else which you may be able to use. I typed this a few days ago and if you can, I really would like for this to be in the book. I would like everyone to know how much I enjoy volunteering. I want people to know how much I want to help people and how important volunteering is to me."

Resume of

William Glenn Hurt

Barren County Circuit Clerk's office/ District Judge John T. Alexander (volunteer) (pass job)

1. Volunteering in Circuit Clerk's office
2. Working in the Drivers License Window
3. Volunteering in District Judge John T. Alexander's office

Cumberland County Public Schools (Volunteer) (Current)

1. College and Career Fair
2. CCMS and CCHS School registration
3. Reality Store
4. Family Learning Night
5. Volunteer Appreciation
6. Veterans' Day Program
7. Christmas Outreach at CCES

Administrative Office of the Courts (Volunteer) (Current)

1. Worked in the Education Department
2. Working in the TS Department
3. Worked in different Departments at AOC
4. Volunteering and Attending the District Judges College, Circuit Judges College, Circuit Clerk College

Cumberland County Justice Center (Volunteer Job) (Current Job)

1. Working in the Circuit Clerk's office
2. Doing computer work
3. Drivers License Window

Columbia-Adair County Chamber of Commerce (Volunteer Job) (Current Job)

1. Making Copies
2. Working on Computer
3. Greeting visitors
4. Attending meetings

Photographer at Cumberland County Middle School (New Volunteer Job) (Current Job)

Taking pictures during and after school also at special events (Volunteer) (Current)

Salaried Job for Attorney Patricia Thomas

Downloading and printing COA Opinions and Board Opinions

Will is a prolific e-mail correspondent. He has over 200 e-mail address and he makes sure to correspond with many of them. His Facebook friends number 1630 and growing. Below are just a few samples. You will notice that they are brief and to the point.

"Dear Sue,

I hope you are having a good day at work today. Is Kathy also having a good day? I am coming to see you sometime and work in my office there. I am in Bowling Green today. NaNa will bring me there to work for you. I have a new PDA which I need to show to you and Kathy."

"Dear NaNa,

I hate to ask you this! I called Mom and told her that I hated to ask you this but she told me that I could tell you. Uncle Joe has a real neat new cell phone and I am sending you the link below. I know that you remember That my Birthday is next month."

Dear NaNa,

I might not be able to sit with you this Sunday because Sarah Sullivan and her boyfriend have asked me to sit with them. They are my friends and will be at church on Sunday. We will be in the balcony. You cab sit in the balcony, too, just maybe on the other side.

Love,

Will"

"Dear Will,

When I brought your lunch to school today, you walked right by me and did not say anything. You could have said, 'Hi NaNa' or 'Thank you, NaNa'. You acted as if you did not even know me. I would not have made you feel embarrassed but I would have felt happy. I felt so sad when you just ignored me.

I love you, NaNa"

"Hi NaNa,

The other day I was at your house. Do you remember when Dr. Bob asked me if I wanted tea to drink. You told him that I did not want any and I would rather have water. Yes, I do like water but it was not nice of you to answer for me. I do not answer for you and you do not answer for me.

Love,

Will Hurt

In 1998, Will's beloved grandfather, Aundie, died while the grandparents were living in England. This was after Will, his parents, brother and sister had enjoyed a wonderful visit there which have given Will wonderful memories.

In 2004, Will's maternal grandmother became concerned about the fifteen year civil war which was raging in the small country on the west coast of Africa. Both grandparents, along with Will's mother, had lived there for a number of years. Both grandparents had taught in a boarding school and his grandmother became very concerned with the plight many of their former students were enduring. She began the long tedious process of bringing the, then twenty-two year old daughter, to the US where she would be safe from starvation, raped or being killed. At the time she had spent one-half of her life surviving by literally running from one refugee camp to another.

In July 2005, Will, along with his family, was at the Atlanta Airport to welcome her to the US and into their family. Lombeh had lost her mother during the long war and soon she was comfortable in her own room in the home of "Mom Marg". Will was thrilled to introduce Lombeh to computers, cell phones, other tech items and take her for long rides in his golf cart.

Lombeh became a welcome addition to Will's family. She has just finished a graduate degree at Lindsey Wilson College in Columbia, Kentucky. Three years later her brother, Burgess, joined our family which has given Will another "big brother" who, when not in school at Lindsey Wilson College, enjoys learning to drive Will's golf cart and his father's large farm truck.

Tributes of praise continue to flow in to this author.

"Will makes me smile, makes me laugh and gives me the ability to see the world differently. He has the biggest heart of anyone I know and gives the best 'just because' hugs. He inspires me and I'm continually amazed by him. Even though I am the older sibling, I look up to him.

Holly Hurt Johnson

Will's Big Sister"

"Will, you have touched my life in so many ways. Your special talents, determination and strong Christian faith are an inspiration to me and everyone else who knows you. You dedication to your family and friends amazes me. You shall always be a special person in my life.

My love,

Alisa Baker"

Evidence below speaks of Will's deep concern for others.

"Hello,

My cousin, Alisa Baker, has just been told that she has breast cancer. She is a great friend and cousin and I ask that you, my friends, pray that this will go away and not return. Please also pray for, Wayne, her husband, and for her daughter, Amber.

Love,

Will"

Will was asked by the author of this book for some of his happy memories. This is his reply.

"I do not remember very much about flying to Disney World and all the fun things we did there. I remember that

Aundie taught me to swim and I sat in the Captain's seat before the plane took off. I do remember when Mom, Dad, Scott, Holly and I went to England to visit my grandparents. I had so much fun and I really liked the big, big rocks. I don't who could put them there. I remember when I would be in school and we would have a big storm. I would become frightened and a student or teacher would come and sit beside me. This always made me feel better."

"I met Will many years before I had the opportunity to have him as a student and I must say the pleasure was and remains all mine. He was always 'tech-savvy' and helped me with many tasks. Will has been an excellent student who demonstrated much personal growth during his educational experiences. He was always willing to challenge himself as he used what was a natural strength to move forward as a student. He became involved in club activities as a freshman which led to his being which led to his being elected to officers' positions as a senior. I was personally encouraged by him on so many occasions. Yes, there were some difficult challenges along the path just as there are for all students; but working with Will was the highlight of my day. He helped me understand his 'techy' world and working together we utilized what we could to solve our own problems at hand. Not all subjects are a strength although quite honestly, this is true for most of us who do not have the same gifts and talents. I am just glad Will gave me the opportunity to support his learning because, as it would go . . . the years may pass, students will come and then move on to other endeavors and I, as a teacher, can only hope to gain from my students the lessons I have learned from Will. It was and shall always be a treasured memory of my year with Will as my student. The young adult he has become is more reward than I could ever ask for as an educator. The changing world is just where Will should be. Our experiences today are so different from those of many years ago and I am grateful that this young man came into the world at just the right time with just the right purpose. He has diligently worked to pursue and create success, which so many will never know because they depend solely on the judgments of those whose opinions are often so inaccurate. I challenge any educator to continue to support Will but more than that to appreciate the differences and embrace the similarities. I have so much respect for this unique young man who will never allow his success to be measured by the number of dollars in his bank account but by the number of days he has volunteered his services to help others.

Ms. Rebekah Burns
Exceptional Education Teacher
Cumberland County High School"

WHO WAS THE TEACHER?

I had the privilege of having Will Hurt in class his freshman year at Cumberland County High School. As the advisor to Family, Career and Community Leaders of America, I encouraged all freshmen to join this student organization and take advantage of the many opportunities it could offer. As Will was an exceptionally quiet student I had no idea I had ignited an interest until his sophomore year. It was then that he not only joined but took an officer position in the CCHS FCCLA chapter. That is when our adventure began.

In the next three years Will not only excelled in all of my classes in which he was enrolled, he excelled in FCCLA. He took full advantage of all the leadership and learning opportunities. He maintained and officer position and traveled with me and fellow FCCLA members to many regional, state and national meeting. Our travels included many trips to Louisville, Kentucky as well as to St. Louis, Missouri and Atlanta, Georgia.

The second semester of his junior year Will competed in Regional FCCLA STAR Events competition. The event which he entered was entitled "Job Application and Interview". He worked very hard to complete a resume, a job application and a letter requesting an interview. He also included letters of reference He won first place and was on his way to State FCCLA STAR Events competition!

The other member and I were nervous on the day of State Competition, but were confident that Will would wow the judges with his perfectly completed folder as well as his executive style, complete with dress shirt and tie. I have never been more proud of a student than when they announced that Will Hurt had indeed placed first in his competition!

To complete Will's adventures in FCCLA and to reward him for winning first place we had the opportunity to travel to Jacksonville, Florida in the fall of his senior year. Two of his fellow senior officers, Cheyanne Wilcoxon and Traci Graves did not want to miss this trip, as they had also worked very hard alongside Will to take to take advantage of the opportunities offered them in FCCLA. That was a trip with many unforgettable memories; running through the Atlanta airport so we would not miss our connecting flight, only to discover that our luggage had, indeed, missed the connecting flight. We were excited to learn that our rental car for the next three days was a beautiful new Dodge Charger. At midnight we found ourselves driving around in circles in Jacksonville looking for our motel. Will and I were delighted as we watched Cheyanne and Traci as they saw the Atlantic Ocean for the first time.

Will taught me so much in the time we spent together. He was always so kind and caring; his spiritual closeness with God was evident. Students are supposed to learn from their teachers. I can only hope Will learned from me because I learned so very much from him.

Mrs. Connie Duvall
Consumer Science Teacher-Retired

This past week found Will fulfilling his volunteer duties at the Kentucky Judicial College. Will volunteered wherever he was needed particularly in the technology area. Many of his friends from the Administrative of the Courts were there and Will was able to visit with his many friends where he served as an intern.

Chief District Judge Vanessa Dickson made this comment, "I first met Will when he was attending Judicial Schools with his father, He has a shy kindness that makes you want to smile whenever you see him. He is always the tech wiz kid teaching us old judges some new tricks with our phones and IPods. He has a way of showing you what to do, with a grin that makes learning fun."

Taped inside the back cover of his grandfather's (Aundie) Bible the author found these words. Surely he wrote them for his grandson William Glenn Hurt.

"Fear not to reach for the stars;

No matter if you fail or fall.

Success will never come to those;

Who fail to reach at all."

Signed: William Glenn Henderson

AFTERWORD

Will's story, his real-life story, is a profound and unifying one. It brings people together in thought, intention, knowledge, hope, love and spirit. It would serve us more "ordinary" humans well to take a page from his book and learn some life-lessons of our own, such as the importance of kindness, fortitude, patience and belief in oneself. The great Chinese philosopher, Lao Tzu must have had this young man in mind when he wrote, "At the center of your being, you have the answer; you know who you are and you know what you want."

Jo Murley
Feature Columnist
Cumberland County News
Burkesville, Kentucky